SALSAS & KETCHUPS

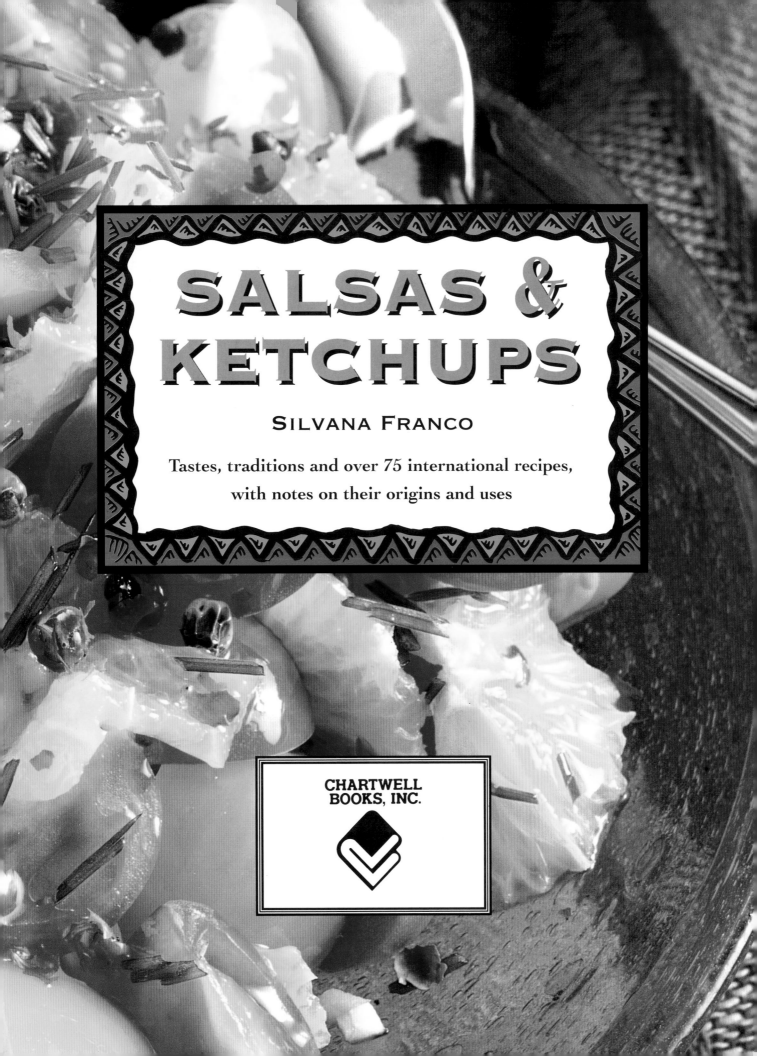

SALSAS & KETCHUPS

SILVANA FRANCO

Tastes, traditions and over 75 international recipes,
with notes on their origins and uses

CHARTWELL
BOOKS, INC.

A QUARTO BOOK

Published by Chartwell Books
A Division of Book Sales Inc.
PO Box 7100
Edison, New Jersey 08818-7100

This edition produced for sale
in the U.S.A., its territories
and dependencies only.

ISBN 0-7858-0350-5

This book was designed and produced by
Quarto Publishing Plc
The Old Brewery
6 Blundell Street
London N7 9BH

Art Director: Moira Clinch
Design: Design Revolution
Senior Art Editor: Liz Brown
Copy Editor: Beverley LeBlanc
Home Economist: Carol Tennent
Picture Researcher: Susannah Jayes
Picture Manager: Giulia Hetherington
Senior Editor: Sian Parkhouse
Editorial Director: Mark Dartford
Photographer: Philip Wilkins
Illustrators: Amanda Green & Andrew Morris

Typeset in Great Britain by Central Southern Typesetters, Eastbourne
Manufactured in Hong Kong by Regent Publishing Services Ltd
Printed in Singapore by Star Standard Industries Pte. Ltd.

CONTENTS

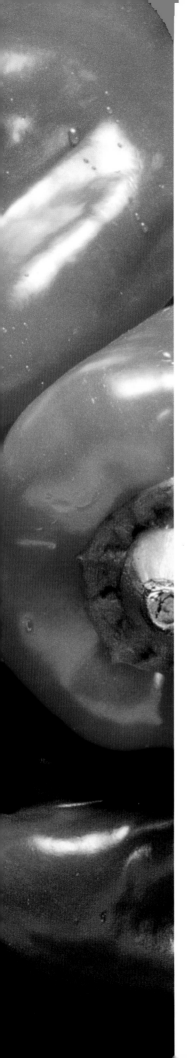

SALSAS *and* KETCHUPS *from* AROUND *the* WORLD

BROKEN INTO SEVEN CHAPTERS, EACH FOCUSING
ON THE CUISINE OF A DIFFERENT AREA OF THE
WORLD, THIS ECLECTIC COLLECTION OF RECIPES
CAPTURES THE ESSENCE OF INDIVIDUAL REGIONS,
WHILE ACKNOWLEDGING THE WORLDWIDE FUSION OF
INGREDIENTS AND COOKING STYLES.

Each chapter contains a selection of recipes
for ketchups, sauces, and salsas, some of
which are based on traditional recipes, while
others are modern interpretations of the
region's style and flavors. All the recipes are
simple to use, and if, as is the case of some
ketchups, cooking time is fairly lengthy, the
preparation is minimal–and the results worth
taking time over. As for the salsas, cooking
times (if any) are, in most cases, well under
30 minutes.

Ketchups and salsas are extremely flexible in
both their ingredients and uses, so once a
recipe has been mastered, experiment with
the spices and ingredients to mix and match
flavors to suit your tastes. Remember, there
are no rules!

From garlic and thyme to cilantro and nutmeg, the flavors of the world add variety and spice to life.

Salsa

Colorful and flavorsome, hot and spicy or cool and refreshing, a salsa is a thing to savor–but what is it? Originating in Mexico, *salsa* simply means "sauce," and in Mexican terms that means fiery and tomatoey with plenty of fresh chilies, onion, cilantro, garlic, and salt. In other parts of the world, however, a salsa is more of a side dish–in Spain, for example, it is served as tapas alongside a handful of other small snacks.

Wherever it is created, however, a salsa is always a blend of chopped, diced, or grated fruit and vegetables, along with fresh herbs characteristic of the region. Sometimes cooked, but most often raw, salsas can be dry, moist, or saucy. But whatever the consistency, they are always served as one element of a meal, either to spice up or cool down the palate.

SERVING SALSAS

WITHOUT DOUBT, THE MOST POPULAR WAY TO SERVE
A SALSA IS AS A DIP. WHETHER AS AN APPETIZER, PART OF A MEAL, OR AS A SNACK, ALMOST ALL
SALSAS CAN BE PUT TO GOOD USE WHEN SERVED WITH A SELECTION OF MORSELS TO DIP WITH.
HERE ARE A FEW SUGGESTIONS OF WHAT TO SERVE WITH YOUR SALSA.

TORTILLA CHIPS

Available in a wide selection of flavors, from cheese-corn chips to fiery nachos, tortilla chips are the best accompaniment to any tomato-based salsa such as Salsa Cruda (page 105) and Instant Tomato Salsa (page 120).

CRUDITES

A selection of crunchy raw vegetables, such as cauliflower flowerets, carrot batons, and sticks of celery make delicious scoops for both creamy and spicy salsas. Prepare the vegetables as close to serving time as possible so they stay crisp.

ROASTED VEGETABLES

Delicious and easy to prepare, roasted vegetables are super for serving with hot or spicy salsas. Simply cut the vegetables into wedges, toss with a little oil and salt and roast at 400°F for 45 minutes to 1 hour. Good choices include fresh plum tomatoes and eggplants, plus all root vegetables, especially parsnips and carrots.

POTATO SKINS

Crispy potato skins are delicious served with creamy salsas, and chili- or onion-based salsas. Try substituting them for the tortilla chips served with the classic South American Salsa Con Queso (page 104). To make your own potato skins, bake 2 large (at least 8-ounce potatoes) for 1 hour, or until soft. Halve the potatoes and scoop out the flesh to leave a shell about ½ inch thick. Cut each half into 6 wedges, then deep-fry in hot vegetable oil for 3 to 5 minutes until crisp and golden. Drain on paper towels and sprinkle lightly with salt or paprika. Serve hot.

CHEESE STRAWS

Buy cheese straws or make your own quickly using 8 ounces thawed puff pastry dough. Lightly flour the countertop and sprinkle generously with freshly grated Parmesan cheese. Roll out the dough onto the surface until it is about ¼ inch thick. Cut into ½-inch wide strips about 6 inches long. Leave the strips flat or twist them a few times to make a rope effect. Brush with a little milk and bake for 15 minutes at 400°F until crisp and golden. Leave to cool and serve warm, or store in an airtight container for 2 or 3 days.

VEGETABLE CHIPS

You can, of course, buy potato chips in a fantastic variety of flavors, but it is very simple to make your own, and, I think, they taste better. Simply peel a large potato, then shave off thin slices with the peeler. Deep-fry these in hot oil for 3 to 4 minutes until they rise to the surface. Scoop them out with a slotted spoon and drain on paper towels before seasoning with salt and, for extra kick, a little ground chili. You can also get some surprisingly good results if you try this method with other root vegetables: carrot, parsnip, sweet potato, celery root, and beet are all delicious when sliced wafer thin and deep-fried. Whatever the vegetable, however, it is best to fry them in batches as they have a tendency to stick together. This applies particularly to starchy vegetables, such as potatoes, which benefit from being soaked in cold water and then dried thoroughly before frying.

In the shady olive groves of Andalusia, in Spain, the succulent fruits gently open.

STORING KETCHUPS

COOKED KETCHUPS WITH A HIGH VINEGAR CONTENT, SUCH AS THE
ENGLISH VARIETIES, CAN BE KEPT FOR AT LEAST SIX MONTHS IF THE BOTTLES ARE CORRECTLY STERILIZED AND
SEALED TO PREVENT FERMENTATION OR THE DEVELOPMENT OF ANY TOXINS. SAFEGUARD KETCHUPS
THAT ARE INTENDED FOR LONG-TERM STORAGE AS FOLLOWS:

1 Preheat the oven to 225°F. Wash the bottles and jars in warm soapy water and rinse well in clean water.

2 Place a wire rack in the bottom of a large saucepan and place the bottles and jars on it, making sure they are not touching each other or the sides of the pan.

Careful storage will ensure that the rich flavors of herbs and spices are not lost.

3 Pour in enough boiling water to cover the bottles, then return the water to a boil and boil rapidly for 10 minutes.

4 Carefully remove the bottles or jars and leave them upside down to drain on a clean towel.

5 Transfer the bottles or jars to the oven to dry out completely. Leave them in the oven until you are ready to fill them with ketchup. Take care not to have the oven temperature any higher than 225°F or there is a danger that the glass will crack.

6 Ladle the hot ketchup into the warm, dry jars, filling them to within ½ inch of the rim. Wipe the rims with a clean, damp cloth, then seal the jars or bottles immediately.

7 Store the ketchups out of direct sunlight in a cool, dry place. Refrigerate once opened.

A pleasing array of jars filled with good things to eat.

BOILING-WATER BATH

It is not essential to boil the ketchups if the jars have been properly sterilized and filled, however, this is an extra safety measure you can do to protect your ketchups. This method heats the contents to a very high temperature, killing off enzymes, which prevents fermentation, and forms a hermetic seal. To ensure a safe seal, use tongs to lower the filled bottles or jars into a large pan of boiling water with a wire rack in the bottom. Boil for 30 minutes, keeping the jar submerged by topping up the pan with boiling water. Carefully remove the jars and leave them to cool for 12 hours. To check the seal, if the jar has a screwtop lid, it will be slightly concave; if you are using a glass-lidded, clip-jar, gently try to lift the lid–if the seal is safe it will resist.

KETCHUP

Always smooth and often spicy, a ketchup is a table condiment that brings a burst of flavor to everyday meals. It is incredibly versatile and can be used to enhance the flavor of any dish– a Jamaican ketchup, for example, tastes superb on an all-American hot dog. There are a number of ways to make ketchup, from the traditional style which contains a high percentage of vinegar and is packed into sterilized jars to be kept for a number of months, to the fresh saucy crossbreeds such as Israeli Sabra (page 40) which need to be kept covered in the refrigerator for only two or three days.

A fine source of flavor, ketchups have been popular for over 300 years.

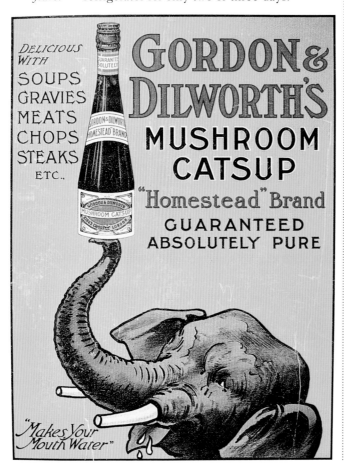

Ketchups have, in fact, been made since the 17th century under the names of *koechiap*, *catchup*, and *catsup*, with the term *ketchup* finally entering the English dictionary about 1710. The most famous ketchup is, of course, the commercially made tomato variety, whose plastic, squeezy bottle full of bright red sauce can be found gracing the kitchen table of homes all around the world. Humble as it is, tomato ketchup brings life to tired food. After all, who would even consider eating a burger and fries without a good old dollop of ketchup on the side? So, imagine what a stir you can cause if you make your own.

What's in a Name?

SALSA IS A GENERAL TERM FOR A
SAUCE, BUT THE FOLLOWING ARE MORE SPECIFIC VARIETIES.

Acar or Ajtar

Fruit or vegetable preserved in, or flavored with, vinegar, spices, and chili.

Blatjang

Thick and chunky blatjangs can be found in southern Africa and Malaysia, and are traditionally flavored with shrimp or shrimp paste.

Catsup

The original ketchup, this term is still used in some regions.

Chowchow

A sour salsa, that generally contains vinegar and spices, and vegetables rather than fruit.

Chutney

A thick ketchup that contains chunks of fruit or vegetables and often whole spices. Thought to have originated in India, chutney is a popular accompaniment to spicy curries.

Ketchup

Thick and smooth fruit or vegetable sauce. Generally contains vinegar as a preservative.

Relish

Fairly impossible to define, every entry here may also be classified as a relish.

Salsa

This translates into sauce, but any small dish made principally from fruit or vegetables, whether raw or cooked, may be called a salsa.

Sambal

Usually a smooth paste. Often quite oily and spicy, but always hot.

PREPARATION TECHNIQUES

Take the plunge –
a top tip for
onion preparation.

PEELING TOMATOES

There are two basic methods for peeling tomatoes. I favor the first technique, mainly because of speed, but there is a noticeable difference in the texture and flavor of the tomato depending upon which method is used. Many other cooks, however, opt for the second method as it is easier to control.

1) Flame–Impale the tomato on a fork or skewer and hold it in a naked flame over a gas ring or under a hot broiler for a few seconds, turning the tomato until the peel blisters. Slip off the peel, and the flesh will still be firm. This method also works well for chilies.

2) Hot Water–Cut a small cross in the top of the tomatoes and place in a bowl. Pour boiling water over and leave for exactly 1 minute. Cool under running cold water, then slip off the peel.

SEEDING TOMATOES

Remove the green stem core and cut the tomatoes in half vertically. Use a teaspoon to scoop out the seeds.

PEELING ONIONS

Plunge whole onions into boiling water for exactly 1 minute. Cool under running water and the skins will soften sufficiently to make peeling very easy.

PEELING GARLIC

If you have more than 2 or 3 garlic cloves to prepare, separate the cloves and remove the outer papery skins. Place the cloves in a small bowl and cover with warm water. Leave for a minute or two, before draining. The skin will soften, and peeling the cloves will be quick and simple.

Pungent garlic adds flavour to both ketchups and salsas, but preparation can be timely.

Roasting peppers brings out their natural sweetness.

ROASTING PEPPERS

Roasted peppers are more often cooked under the broiler, rather than actually roasted in an oven. Although it is quicker to halve or quarter the peppers before roasting them, it is much better to keep them whole so the delicious juices which are released during broiling or roasting are collected inside the pepper.

Arrange the whole peppers on a baking sheet or broiler pan and place under a preheated broiler for 8 to 12 minutes, turning until the skin is blistered and blackened. Cover with a clean dish towel or place in a plastic bag for about 5 minutes so that the steam helps lift up the skin. Then pierce a hole in the bottom of the pepper and squeeze out the juice. Save the juice to add to a dressing or marinade for the peppers. Peel away the skins and halve the peppers. Remove the central cores and seeds.

SEEDING CHILIES

Use a small sharp knife to halve the chilies lengthwise then, with the tip of the knife, scrape away the seeds and white membrane. If you are sensitive to the pungent oils of some chilies, you may find it easier to scrape the seeds out under cold running water.

SNIPPING CHIVES

Don't bother to chop chives in the way that you do other herbs. Instead, gather up a small bunch and quickly snip them with a pair of sharp kitchen scissors.

TOASTING SEEDS AND NUTS

Most nuts, seeds, and some spices, in particular cumin, benefit from toasting because the dry heat really brings out the flavor. My preferred method is to stir-fry the ingredient in a large nonstick skillet, without any oil, for between 2 and 5 minutes until it turns golden and releases its aroma.

Chopped or flaked nuts may also be placed under a hot broiler or in a hot oven for a few minutes until golden, with the latter method giving the most even coloring.

SEEDING AVOCADOS

Cut the avocado in half lengthwise, cutting right through to the seed. Hold the avocado in both hands and twist in opposite directions, while pulling the two halves apart. Hold the half

Fiery chilies need careful handling, even when they are dried.

containing the seed in one hand and pierce the seed firmly with a sharp knife. Lift up the knife and the seed will come away with it.

CUTTING CORN KERNELS

Remove the kernels from a corn cob either before or after cooking, depending upon your use–leave the kernels on the cob for barbecuing but cut them off before boiling.

Strip off the green husky leaves and silky threads. Slice off the stem at the bottom. Hold the cob upright on a board, and, using a large sharp knife, slice down; the kernels will slice off easily.

GRINDING SEEDS AND PASTES

The traditional way to grind hard seeds, or pound moist ingredients into a paste, is by using a mortar and pestle. They can be made from a number of materials, but are often porcelain or marble. The end of the pestle and the bottom of the mortar are usually unglazed or slightly coarse to create friction between the two. Of course, anyone in a hurry can always use a mini food processor.

A mortar and pestle is indispensable when crushing small seed pods.

Bread Sticks

Rich pickings: sun-ripened tomatoes make the perfect salsa base.

Italian-style *grissini*, or bread sticks, are a super crisp snack for serving with every kind of salsa. Readily available from grocery stores, they now come in a number of thicknesses and flavors, such as sesame seed and cheese. But if you want to make them yourself, here is a simple recipe.

MAKES 30

2 cups bread flour, plus	*1 tsp salt*
extra for rolling	*½ cup warm water*
¼ ounce quick-rise active	*(120°F)*
dry yeast	*2 tbsp olive oil*

❶ Preheat the oven to 450°F. Sift the flour and salt into a bowl. Stir in the yeast and make a well in the center.

❷ Add the water and olive oil and bring together to make a firm dough. Knead for 5 minutes until smooth.

❸ Rub a little oil into the surface of the dough. Cover with a clean dish towel and leave to rise in a warm place for 40 minutes.

❹ Knead the dough lightly, then roll it out on a floured surface to make a rectangle about 6 inches wide and ¼ inch thick. Cut the rectangle widthwise into 30 thin strips.

❺ Roll each strip into a long, thin rope about 10 inches long. Arrange on a baking sheet and bake for 15 minutes until crisp and golden. Allow to cool, then store in an airtight container.

EUROPE

OF ALL THE REGIONS *covered in this book, Europe, and in particular England, has the most extensive collection of traditional ketchups, some of which can be traced back hundreds of years to ancient recipes. On the whole, these sauces tend to be an uncomplicated blend of only two or three main ingredients simmered in a spiced vinegar solution, which, if stored correctly, will keep for a number of months.*

When it comes to salsas, however, the flavors of the Mediterranean come into their own with Greek olives and feta cheese, Italian plum tomatoes, fresh oregano and olive oils, and French mustard and garlic, making warm, summer-tasting salsa combinations.

European Ingredients

A colorful array of freshly picked produce in a Venician open-air market.

Balsamic vinegar

Made only in one region of northern Italy, traditional balsamic vinegar is aged in oak casks for 10 to 20 years to produce a dark, syrupy vinegar that is sweet enough to be served straight from the bottle as a salad dressing. Although fairly pricy, just a small splash enlivens tomato salsas, broiled fish, and vegetables, and brings a new dimension to almost any vinegar-based ketchup.

Olives

All olives we buy and eat have been cured, as they are very bitter if eaten straight from the tree. Green olives are picked and pickled before they are ripe, and are best served as a cocktail appetizer, and as such can be bought packed with delicious stuffings such as pimiento, garlic, and almonds. Black ripe olives are more suitable for cooking with, and often grace pizzas and pasta sauces, as well as salads and salsas. Greek, French, and Italian olives, as

well as ones from California, are equally popular.
But whichever type you buy, especially if you buy
them loose rather than packed in brine or oil, keep
them in the refrigerator and eat within 3 days.

OREGANO

Closely related to French marjoram, but rather
more powerful, Italian oregano is, according to
some, best when dried. Alongside basil, it is the herb
most associated with Italian cooking and
is an essential flavoring of the classic tomato
sauce used for both pasta and pizzas.

MUSTARD

Most of the mustards available are now made from
ground brown mustard seed, as opposed to the
once-popular, and much hotter, black seeds. Often
the seeds are only partly ground, resulting in the
mild, coarse-grained varieties that are currently so
fashionable. There are many specialized mustards
sold, such as Dijon and tarragon, which are most
often served with meats but can also be stirred into
simple vinaigrettes, mayonnaises, and soft cheese to
make delicious dressings.

TOMATOES

With so many varieties of tomatoes available it is
difficult to know which to choose. Unfortunately,
many are grown for appearance, rather than
flavor, and are often watery and bland. If you can,

*A French market
stall displays its
wonderfully fragrant
spices.*

buy ripe, Italian plum tomatoes or the much
smaller sweet cherry tomatoes.
Avoid the large,
hothouse type that
look so perfect and
appetizing, as the
flavor, or lack of
it, will probably
be disappointing.
Keep an eye open for
yellow tomatoes, which
not only look good but taste
delicious, too.

DRIED TOMATO SALSA

This is the most time-consuming salsa in the book, because first you must dry the tomatoes (see right). Dry them in large batches and store in plain, top-quality olive oil until you are ready to use them–don't, however, be tempted to flavor the oil with any herbs as it will detract from the pure flavor of the tomatoes. Drying them really brings out the sweetness in all varieties of tomatoes, and they can then be used to enhance a whole host of dishes, such as salsas, salads, risottos–my absolute favorite way to use them is on a freshly baked mozzarella-covered pizza topped with a handful of torn basil leaves.

Serve this sunny-tasting Italian salsa with a bowl of ripe olives, a slab of Gorgonzola cheese, and some warm garlic bread for a rustic first course or an alfresco lunch.

SERVES 2

12 home-dried tomato halves, roughly chopped (see below)
2 purple shallots, finely chopped
2 garlic cloves, finely chopped

handful roughly torn basil leaves
3 tbsp olive oil
2 tbsp balsamic vinegar
salt

Toss all the ingredients together with salt to taste in a bowl and serve within about 2 hours. This is best eaten at room temperature.

TO DRY TOMATOES

The idea is to dry the tomatoes, not cook them, so keep an eye on them while they are in the oven, turning them occasionally and removing any that are ready before the others. They will shrivel up but should still be soft and not too papery. Because of the different sizes of tomatoes and performances of individual ovens, the process can take anything from 6 to 10 hours.

Dry as many tomatoes as you can fit into your oven at one time. In my oven, I find 20 tomatoes is about right. If you want to store the dried tomatoes in olive oil, layer them in sterilized jars, cover with the oil, seal, and store for up to 6 months.

INGREDIENTS

tomatoes
kosher salt

extra-virgin olive oil for bottling

❶ Preheat the oven to its lowest setting. Rinse the tomatoes well and cut them in half. Scoop out the seeds and discard.
❷ Place the tomatoes cut-side down on paper towels for 10 to 15 minutes to remove the excess moisture.
❸ Lightly sprinkle the inside of the tomato halves with salt and arrange them closely, but not touching, on 2 wire racks, cut sides down. Transfer to the oven.
❹ If your oven allows it, keep the door slightly ajar by propping it open with a metal skewer.

Dried Tomato Salsa

RHUBARB KETCHUP

Keep this stored in a cool, dark place for at least a month before using to let the flavors mature.

MAKES ABOUT 1¾ QUARTS

2 pounds fresh rhubarb
¼ cup freshly squeezed orange juice
2 large onions, roughly chopped
4½ cups white vinegar
4 cups light brown sugar

1 tsp salt
1 tsp allspice berries
1 tsp black or brown mustard seeds
1 tsp black peppercorns

❶ Rinse the rhubarb stalks well, then cut them into 1-inch pieces. Place in a large saucepan with the orange juice, onions, vinegar, sugar, salt, and spices.

❷ Heat slowly, stirring until the sugar dissolves. Cover and simmer over the lowest heat for 1½ hours until the mixture is pulpy, stirring occasionally.

❸ Strain the mixture through a fine nonmetallic strainer, then pour immediately into hot, sterilized bottles. Seal (page 10) and store.

ENGLISH ORCHARD APPLE KETCHUP

Use a small, flavorsome variety of apple for this ketchup: Crispins, Golden Delicious, and Winesap are very good choices, but you can make use of whatever type you have available.

MAKES ABOUT 5 CUPS

*4 pounds apples, cored and
    roughly chopped
1 large onion, roughly chopped
2½ cups white vinegar*

*1 tbsp salt
1 tsp whole cloves
1 cinnamon stick
1 cup sugar*

❶ Place the apples, onion, salt, cloves, cinnamon, and vinegar in a large pan. Bring to a boil, then cover and simmer for 1½ hours, stirring occasionally, until pulpy.

❷ Strain through a fine nonmetallic strainer, then return to the pan and put over low heat. Stir in the sugar until it dissolves. Bring to a boil and boil rapidly for 5 minutes, then immediately pour into hot, sterilized bottles. Seal (page 10) and store.

SPANISH ONION SALSA

If you don't have the large, mild-tasting Spanish onions to hand, use 2 regular onions in place of each Spanish one.

SERVES 6

*2 tbsp butter
2 tbsp olive oil
4 Spanish onions, thickly sliced
2 tbsp capers*

*4 anchovies in oil, roughly
    chopped
2 tbsp red-wine vinegar
2 tbsp chopped fresh parsley
seasoning*

❶ Melt the butter with the oil in a large pan and add the onions. Cook very slowly for 20 to 30 minutes until softened and golden brown.

❷ Transfer to a serving dish and stir in the capers, anchovies, vinegar, and parsley.

❸ Season to taste and serve warm or at room temperature. Do not refrigerate.

French Mustard Salsa

Make this salsa up to one day in advance and store in the refrigerator until ready to serve.

SERVES 4

8 ounces thin French-style
   beans, trimmed
1 cup blanched whole almonds

2 tbsp walnut oil
1 tbsp white-wine vinegar
1 tbsp wholegrain mustard
salt

❶ Cut the beans into 1-inch pieces and blanch in a pan of boiling salted water for 3 to 5 minutes until just tender. Drain in a colander, then cool under cold running water. Drain well on paper towels.
❷ Place the almonds in a heated wok or skillet and stir-fry for a few minutes until golden. Place in bowl with the beans.
❸ Whisk together the oil, vinegar, mustard, and a little salt, then toss together with the beans and nuts. Transfer to a bowl and leave to cool, then cover and chill until required.

Roasted Garlic Salsa

Don't be put off by the quantity of garlic involved in this salsa–the slow roasting mellows the pungency of the cloves, producing a melt-in-the-mouth sweetness. Serve this salsa with toasted, country-style bread and a simple tomato salad for a sophisticated appetizer.

SERVES 4

4 garlic bulbs
2 rosemary sprigs
6 tbsp olive oil
2 tbsp chopped fresh sage

2 tbsp chopped fresh flat-leaf
   parsley
kosher salt

❶ Preheat the oven to 325°F. Place the garlic bulbs and rosemary sprigs in a roasting pan and drizzle with 4 tbsp of the oil and ¼ cup water.
❷ Sprinkle with a little salt and roast for 45 minutes, until the cloves are very soft. Cover the pan with foil if the bulbs start to become too brown.
❸ Leave the bulbs to cool for a few minutes, then carefully squeeze the whole cloves out of their papery skins. Put in a bowl and toss with the chopped herbs and remaining olive oil. Serve warm or at room temperature.

French Mustard Salsa

ITALIAN KETCHUP

This mouthwatering ketchup tastes particularly good with char-grilled fish.

MAKES ABOUT 5 CUPS

*1 large eggplant, roughly
    chopped*
*6 large ripe tomatoes, roughly
    chopped*
*1 cooking apple, cored and
    roughly chopped*
1 large onion, roughly chopped

2 garlic cloves, halved
¾ cup red-wine vinegar
1 cup soft brown sugar
5 star anise
handful fresh basil leaves
1 tsp salt

❶ Place the eggplant, tomatoes, apple, onion, garlic, vinegar, sugar, star anise, basil, and salt in a large saucepan.
❷ Bring to a boil, then lower the heat, cover, and simmer for 1½ hours until thick and pulpy, stirring occasionally.
❸ Strain the mixture through a fine nonmetallic strainer, then immediately pour into hot, sterilized bottles. Seal (page 10) and store.

MUSHROOM KETCHUP

This is a versatile condiment and ingredient and can be added to soups and gravies for extra flavor, or used in place of soy sauce in stir-fries and rice dishes. If decanted into sealed and sterilized bottles, this ketchup will keep for a number of months; see page 10 for details on storage.

MAKES ABOUT 2½ CUPS

2 pounds large, fresh
  mushrooms
2¾ tbsp salt
2½ cups red-wine vinegar
1 tbsp ground allspice

½-inch piece gingerroot, roughly
  chopped
2 mace blades
1 shallot, finely chopped

❶ Layer the mushrooms and salt in a lidded preserving jar. Close the lid and leave for 2 days, stirring twice each day.
❷ Empty the contents of the jar into a large saucepan with the remaining ingredients. Cover and simmer for 30 minutes, stirring occasionally. Strain the mixture through a fine nonmetallic strainer, then immediately pour into hot, sterilized bottles. Seal (page 10) and store.

MEDITERRANEAN SALSA

Serve this Mediterranean salsa warm
or at room temperature as part of a meal, or toss it
into a pan of freshly cooked pasta to make a super light
lunch or supper dish.

SERVES 4

1 large eggplant
4 long shallots
2 plum tomatoes
1 tbsp olive oil
salt and freshly ground
  black pepper

FOR THE DRESSING
3 tbsp olive oil
juice of ½ lemon
1 tbsp chopped fresh oregano

❶ Preheat the broiler to high. Slice the eggplant into ½-inch
slices. Quarter the shallots and tomatoes, then place on a
foil-lined broiler pan with the eggplant. Brush with olive oil
and sprinkle lightly with salt.

❷ Place the vegetables under the broiler for 8 to 10
minutes, turning once, until tender and lightly charred. Cut
the eggplant slices into cubes and place in a large bowl with
the shallots and tomatoes.

❸ Quickly whisk together the dressing ingredients and
pour over the warm vegetables. Toss together and season to
taste.

BRAMBLE KETCHUP

This is a great way to make good use of leftover summer fruit such as blackberries and raspberries, and tastes superb served with cheddar cheese and country-style bread. Make sure the cheese you pair it with is sharp and robust, or the flavors of the ketchup will take over. If you prefer a completely smooth ketchup, use whole spices and after cooking, strain the ketchup through a fine nonmetallic strainer.

MAKES ABOUT 5 CUPS
2 quarts blackberries
4 cups white sugar
2½ cups white-wine vinegar
1 tsp ground cloves
1 tsp ground allspice
1 cinnamon stick

❶ Place the blackberries, sugar, vinegar, and spices in a pan. Bring to a boil, stirring until the sugar dissolves. Cover and simmer gently for 1 hour.
❷ Remove the cinnamon stick, then immediately pour the mixture into hot, sterilized bottles. Seal (page 10) and store.

Ripe Olive
and Plum Tomato Salsa

For a delicious appetizer or light supper dish, place a ½-inch thick slice of rinded soft goat cheese on a thick slice of country bread. Broil until it is bubbling and golden, then serve immediately with a big spoonful of this fragrant salsa on the side.

SERVES 4

6 plum tomatoes, roughly diced
5 ounces Kalamata olives, left whole
6 scallions, thinly sliced
2 tbsp olive oil
1 tbsp balsamic vinegar
1 garlic clove, finely chopped
1 tbsp chopped fresh basil
salt and freshly ground black pepper

❶ Place the tomatoes and olives in a serving bowl and toss together. Sprinkle the scallions over.
❷ Whisk together the olive oil, balsamic vinegar, garlic, basil, and plenty of seasoning. Drizzle over the salsa and serve immediately.

THE MIDDLE EAST

FROM A CULINARY POINT *of view, the Middle East not only covers the southern Asia region, stretching from Turkey down to Yemen, but also encapsulates the northern African countries of Morocco, Algeria, Libya, and Egypt. The food is hearty and well balanced with grains, beans, and legumes forming the staples of the diet. Although flavorsome ingredients such as tahini paste, made from sesame seeds, dried fruit, olives, nuts, garlic, and yogurt all feature strongly, spicy hot food does not play a key role in the cooking of the region, and the use of the chili is relatively minimal.*

Street food is very popular, with vendors selling local specialties, such as flat bread packed with onion salsa, or two or three falafel (fried garbanzo bean patties) splashed with a spicy sauce.

MIDDLE EASTERN INGREDIENTS

Everyday life for the vendors in this Egyptian street bazaar.

CORIANDER

Both the seed and leaf of this herb are edible, and you will also see the leaf called cilantro. Found all over the Middle East, particularly in Morocco, the small seeds are round and hard, and, like cumin, are available both whole and ground. I recommend, however, that you buy only the whole seeds and pound them lightly in a mortar with a pestle just before using.

As a fresh leaf, cilantro has an aromatic flavor that can be matched with almost anything. Pick the leaves from the stem and toss them whole or roughly chopped into a raw salsa, or stir into cooked sauces toward the end of the cooking time. It is used extensively in the Middle East in dishes such as couscous.

CUMIN SEEDS

A favorite flavoring in northern Africa, cumin also appears extensively in Asian cooking. A small seed, it is sold both whole and ground, and like most spices should be roasted, toasted, or fried, rather than added raw to a dish. Cumin has a subtle flavor and can be used generously.

OLIVE OIL

Not only a favorite Mediterranean ingredient, olive oil is extensively used in the Middle East as well. Extra-virgin olive oil is from the first pressing of the olives and is therefore the purest and most flavorsome variety. It is also the most expensive–by quite a margin–of all types of olive oil, with many given labels such as simply olive oil, light olive oil, or pure olive oil. These oils have been refined more and have less character than the extra- virgin, but are fine for cooking with. Save your special top-quality, extra-virgin olive oil for raw salsas and salad dressings, as a high temperature, such as that required for frying, destroys most of the flavor which you have paid extra for.

TAHINI PASTE

This thick, oily paste is simply crushed sesame seeds. Usually packed into a glass jar, it separates during storage and needs a stiff beating before use. An essential ingredient in many Middle Eastern dishes such as hummus and falafel, tahini paste is also delicious added to ketchups, soups, and stocks.

YOGURT

Yogurt is an important ingredient in the Middle East. Often used as the base in marinades and soups, it adds a refreshing tang to otherwise bland dishes. Plain yogurt is usually made from cows' milk which live bacteria cultures are added to, and it is widely available.

Spices have always played a major role in Middle Eastern cuisine.

FATTOUSH

This traditional Lebanese salsa has pieces of
crisply toasted Middle Eastern flat bread, such as pita,
tossed in just before serving.

SERVES 4-6

1 cucumber, diced
1 large red bell pepper, cored,
  seeded, and diced
4 ripe tomatoes, diced
2½ ounces full-flavored black
  olives, such as any oily Greek
  or Spanish variety
bunch scallions, thickly sliced on
  the diagonal

2 tbsp chopped fresh flat-leaf
  parsley
2 pita breads, toasted until
  crisp and golden
juice of ½ lemon
3 tbsp olive oil
salt and freshly ground black
  pepper

❶ Toss together the cucumber, pepper, tomatoes, olives,
onions, and parsley in a large bowl.
❷ Break the pitas into bite-sized pieces and add to the salsa.
❸ Whisk together the lemon juice, olive oil, and plenty of
seasoning. Pour over the salad, toss together, and serve
immediately.

SABRA

This Israeli dish is a cross between a ketchup
and a salsa. It is often included as a dip with crackers and
bread or part of a *mezze*, a selection of small dishes served
together as a first course.

SERVES 2

1 ripe avocado
1 green, bell pepper, cored,
  seeded, and finely diced
1 small onion, finely diced
2 tbsp white-wine vinegar

1 tbsp fresh lemon juice
¾ cup plain yogurt
salt and freshly ground black
  pepper

❶ Halve, skin, and seed the avocado, then, in a large bowl,
mash it until it is smooth.
❷ Add the pepper, onion, vinegar, lemon juice, and yogurt to
the avocado and stir together, making sure the avocado is well
coated.
❸ Season to taste. Cover and chill until ready to serve.

Harissa

This condiment is used in northern Africa, particularly in Morocco, where a small amount is always served on the side with couscous. If you prefer, mix it with a smooth tomato sauce to make a less-powerful ketchup.

SERVES 10

10 fresh red chilies
1 red bell pepper
4 garlic cloves, roughly chopped
1 tsp ground cumin

1 tsp coriander seeds
1 tsp kosher salt
3 tbsp white-wine vinegar
2 tbsp olive oil

❶ Seed and roughly chop the chilies and pepper.
❷ Place the chilies and peppers in a mortar with the garlic, ground cumin, and coriander seeds, then grind to a paste with the pestle; you can use a food processor if you prefer.
❸ Stir in the salt, vinegar, and olive oil, then cover and keep in the refrigerator for up to a week. This freezes well.

Tahini Sauce

This sauce is used at Middle Eastern dining tables and as a flavoring in countless dishes. Mix it with plain yogurt to make a creamy dip for crudités or potato chips.

SERVES 6

2 garlic cloves, roughly chopped
⅔ cup tahini (sesame) paste
½ tsp ground coriander
½ tsp ground cumin
juice of 1 lemon
salt and freshly ground black
  pepper

❶ Place the garlic, tahini paste, coriander, and cumin in a blender or food processor. Whiz together for a minute, then, with the motor running, gradually add the lemon juice and ¼ cup water.

❷ Season well. Transfer to a glass jar or plastic tub and seal, then chill until ready to serve. This will keep in the refrigerator for up to 10 days.

Fried Garlic *and* Garbanzo Salsa

Serve this salsa with a selection of salads as part of a meal, or toss with a little plain yogurt and eat with pita bread for a delicious light lunch.

SERVES 4 TO 6

2 tbsp vegetable oil
2 garlic cloves, thinly sliced
1 tsp cumin seeds
2 cups canned garbanzo beans,
  drained and rinsed

2 tbsp chopped fresh mint
2 tbsp chopped fresh cilantro
juice of 1 lime
salt and freshly ground black
  pepper

❶ Heat the oil in a small skillet, then slowly cook the garlic and cumin seeds for 5 minutes, stirring occasionally, until the garlic is softened but not colored.
❷ Place the garbanzo beans in a bowl and stir in the fried garlic mixture, chopped mint and cilantro, and the lime juice.
❸ Season to taste and serve while still warm, or cover and chill until required.

ZHOUG

Also known as *zhoog* or *zhug*, this is a hot condiment from Yemen, where chilies are very popular. Spoon it into soups and dips or drizzle it over falafel (fried garbanzo-bean patties). It can be kept in the refrigerator for up to 10 days, but is most pungent the day it is made.

SERVES 10

6 garlic cloves, roughly chopped
6 green chilies, seeded, and
    roughly chopped
2 tomatoes, peeled, seeded, and
    roughly chopped
8 tbsp chopped fresh flat-leaf
    parsley

8 tbsp chopped fresh cilantro
1 tbsp ground cumin
2 tbsp olive oil
2 tbsp lemon juice
salt and freshly ground black
    pepper

❶ Place the garlic and chilies in a blender or food processor and whiz until well blended.
❷ Add the tomatoes, parsley, cilantro, and cumin and whiz again. With the motor running, slowly pour in the olive oil and lemon juice to make a smooth, thick sauce.
❸ Season well. Transfer to a glass jar or plastic tub and seal, then chill for at least an hour before serving.

EGGPLANT *AND* TAHINI
KETCHUP

Barbecues are very popular throughout the Middle East and this sauce is served as a fantastic accompaniment to grilled or broiled vegetables, chicken, and meat. Stored in the refrigerator, covered, it will keep for 2 to 3 days.

SERVES 4

1 large eggplant, halved
lengthwise
2 tbsp olive oil
2 tbsp tahini (sesame) paste

2 garlic cloves, crushed
juice of ½ lemon
2 tbsp chopped fresh cilantro
salt and freshly ground black
pepper

❶ Preheat the broiler or light the barbecue. Broil or barbecue the eggplant halves for about 30 minutes, turning once until softened.
❷ Peel and discard the skin from the eggplant. Purée the flesh in a blender or food processor and transfer to a bowl. Stir in the olive oil, tahini paste, garlic, lemon juice, and cilantro. Season well.

SPICY ORANGE SALSA

You'll find this zesty salsa served alongside
grilled fish and meat in Turkey. It tastes best served
at room temperature.

SERVES 4

3 large oranges, peeled and
*   segmented*
1 red onion, finely chopped
1 firm tomato, deseeded, and
*   cut into tiny dice*

FOR THE DRESSING
2 tbsp olive oil
2 tbsp red wine vinegar
1 tsp chilli powder
2 tbsp chopped fresh thyme
salt and freshly ground black
*   pepper*

❶ Cut each orange segment into 3 even, bite-sized pieces,
then place them in a serving bowl with the onion and tomato
and gently toss together.
❷ Whisk together the dressing ingredients with a fork until
well blended. Season to taste and pour over the salsa.
❸ Toss the salsa together well, cover and leave to rest for 1–4
hours, until ready to serve.

FETA *AND* OLIVE SALSA

For a simple, tasty lunch, pile the
salsa on top of thick slices of toasted bread and drizzle
with the lemon-oil dressing.

SERVES 2

1 large ripe avocado, cubed
2 large ripe tomatoes, cubed
100g • 4oz black olives
1 red onion, roughly chopped
100g • 4oz feta cheese, cubed

1 tbsp chopped fresh parsley
2 tbsp olive oil
juice of a lemon
seasoning

❶ Place the avocado, tomatoes, olives, onion and feta in a
serving bowl and toss well together.
❷ Whisk together the parsley, olive oil, lemon juice and
seasoning and drizzle over the feta salsa. Serve immediately.

TABBOULEH

This classic Lebanese dish is made with bulgur wheat, also labeled as cracked wheat. It is sold precooked and dried so it simply needs rehydrating with boiling water.

SERVES 4 TO 6

⅔ cup bulgur wheat
2 tomatoes, chopped
2 garlic cloves, finely chopped
1 red onion, finely chopped
⅔ cup crumbled or diced
   feta cheese
4 tbsp chopped fresh mint
juice of 1 lemon
3 tbsp olive oil
salt and freshly ground black
   pepper

❶ Put the bulgur wheat in a large bowl and cover with boiling water; set aside for 20 minutes until the grains swell and absorb most of the water. Drain very well, squeezing out any excess moisture with your hands. Return to the bowl.
❷ Stir in the tomatoes, garlic, onion, feta cheese, mint, lemon juice, and olive oil. Mix together, season to taste, and serve. Cover and chill until ready to serve.

APRICOT DUKKAH

Dukkah is a nutty Egyptian dish that is sold by street vendors in little paper cones. I've added dried apricots and a few extra spices to turn it into a savory salsa that can be kept in an airtight container for a number of weeks. For added piquancy, stir in a little lemon juice, chopped red onion, and garlic when you are ready to serve.

SERVES 4 TO 6

1 cup roughly chopped hazelnuts
4 tbsp sesame seeds
1 tsp coriander seeds
1 tsp cumin seeds

1 tbsp chopped fresh thyme
1 tbsp chopped fresh mint
1 cup roughly chopped ready-to-eat dried apricots
salt and freshly ground black pepper

❶ Place the nuts, sesame seeds, coriander seeds, and cumin seeds in a large, heated skillet or wok and stir-fry for 5 to 10 minutes until the nuts and seeds are golden.
❷ Transfer the nuts and seeds to a food processor with the thyme and mint and half of the apricots. Pulse together until finely chopped and crumbly.
❸ Transfer the mixture to a bowl. Stir in the remaining pieces of apricot and season to taste.

AFRICA

DIFFERENT COUNTRIES AND REGIONS *of Africa* each have varied culinary characteristics. In certain areas there are limited food resources – whether the country has suffered a natural disaster or has poor-quality land. In other areas, however, the food is hearty, wholesome, healthy, and very tasty. Not unlike the rest of the world, Africa is absorbing the flavors of many other countries, such as those from South America, and producing a style of food that is now every bit as innovative as that found in the other major continents.

AFRICAN INGREDIENTS

An African market provides plenty of fresh, delicious produce.

OKRA

Also known as ladies fingers, bhindi, okro, and ochroes, this green, finger-shaped vegetable plays a key role in the cooking of many African, Caribbean, and Asian countries. If not cooked thoroughly, however, it has a tendency toward stickiness which can make a dish unpleasant to eat. Before cooking, wash and dry it carefully, then trim off the ends. Okra is especially good stewed with other vegetables, as in the classic gumbo from Louisiana.

PALM OIL

Only available in specialist stores, palm oil is a bright-red oil with a very distinct flavor. Use it in small quantities to enhance soups, salsas, and

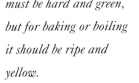

sauces. If you do not have access to any, use ordinary sunflower or corn oil with a little turmeric added for flavor and color.

PLANTAIN

Even though it is a member of the banana family, a plantain cannot be eaten raw. Instead it should be fried, boiled, or baked. Plantains, however, can be used at any stage of ripeness from green through to black, and, like bananas, they become sweeter as they ripen. To make crisp plantain chips, the plantain must be hard and green, but for baking or boiling it should be ripe and yellow.

The bright, jewel-like colors of these African spices provide a stunning display.

FRESH SHRIMP SALSA

This simple salsa makes a wonderful snack. If you have difficulty sourcing palm oil, use vegetable oil and add 1 tsp ground turmeric.

SERVES 4

2 tbsp palm oil
1 small onion, finely chopped
2 fresh red chilies, seeded and finely chopped
4 garlic cloves, finely chopped
2 tomatoes, peeled, seeded, and diced

10 ounces fresh small shrimp, shelled
½ cup chopped fresh cilantro
juice of 1 lime
salt and freshly ground black pepper

❶ Heat the oil in a pan and slowly fry the onion, chilies, and garlic for about 5 minutes, stirring occasionally, until softened.
❷ Stir in the tomatoes, shrimp, cilantro, and lime juice and continue frying slowly for 3 to 4 minutes longer, stirring occasionally until the shrimp turn pink. Season to taste and serve warm or at room temperature.

AFRICAN EGGPLANT DIP

This creamy sauce is a specialty of northern Africa. Serve it at room temperature with hot toast for a tasty appetizer.

SERVES 6

4 tbsp olive oil
1 large eggplant, diced
1 onion, roughly chopped
2 garlic cloves, roughly chopped
1 red chili, seeded and finely chopped
1 tsp ground cumin

¼ tsp turmeric
3 tomatoes, roughly chopped
freshly squeezed juice of 1 lime
2 tbsp chopped fresh parsley
salt and freshly ground black pepper
plain yogurt, to serve

❶ Fry the eggplant in 3 tbsp oil for 5 minutes on each side until tender and golden. Remove with a slotted spoon and drain well on paper towels.
❷ Heat the remaining oil in the same pan. Add the onion, garlic, and chili and slowly cook, stirring occasionally, for 3 minutes. Add the cumin and turmeric and cook for 2 minutes longer, until the onions are softened.
❸ Stir in the tomatoes, lime juice, parsley, and eggplant chunks and cook very slowly for 15 minutes, mashing down with a fork until thick and pulpy. Season to taste. Leave to cool, then chill until ready to serve with plain yogurt.

Fresh Shrimp Salsa

OKRA SALSA

Here's a spicy salsa that makes a super accompaniment to smoked meats and seafood. If you wish, add a handful of cooked, shelled shrimp.

SERVES 6

4 tbsp palm oil
2 cups sliced okra
2 onions, finely chopped
½-inch piece gingerroot, finely grated
1 red chili, seeded and finely chopped
2 garlic cloves, finely chopped
1 tsp apple pie spice
½ tsp turmeric
2 tomatoes, peeled, seeded, and diced
2 tbsp chopped fresh cilantro
salt and freshly ground black pepper

❶ Heat the oil in a large saucepan. Add the okra, onions, ginger, chili, garlic, and spices and stir-fry for 5 minutes. Add the tomatoes and 3 tbsp water, cover, and simmer for 15 minutes until the okra is tender.
❷ Stir in the cilantro and season to taste. Serve hot.

TANGY ORANGE KETCHUP

This ketchup makes a superb accompaniment
and works well as a marinade or glaze for roasted,
broiled, or barbecued fish and chicken. For a sweeter
ketchup, peel the fruit before using.

MAKES ABOUT 5 CUPS

2 oranges
4 limes
8 garlic cloves
2 red chilies, seeded and finely
    chopped
2 to 2¼ cups soft brown sugar

2 cups cider vinegar
2 cups apple juice
1 tsp salt
8 whole cloves
8 whole black peppercorns
2 red bell peppers, seeded and
    diced

❶ Roughly chop the oranges and limes without peeling them. Place them in a large saucepan with the garlic, chilies, sugar, vinegar, apple juice, salt, cloves, and peppercorns. Bring to a boil, stirring until the sugar dissolves.

❷ Cover and simmer for 45 minutes. Add the peppers and simmer for 45 minutes longer until the fruit is soft and pulpy. Strain the mixture through a fine nonmetallic strainer, then pour immediately into hot, sterilized bottles. Seal (page 10) and store.

FRIED PLANTAIN SALSA

Fried plantain chips make a delicious snack in their own right, but remember if you are eating them plain to season them before frying. This tasty salsa cannot wait around to be eaten as the fried plantain soften fairly rapidly.

SERVES 6

2 large, under-ripe plantains
vegetable oil for frying
2 tomatoes, diced
1 mango, peeled and diced
4 scallions, finely chopped
FOR THE DRESSING
1 garlic clove, finely chopped

2 tbsp cider vinegar
2 tbsp vegetable oil
few drops hot-pepper sauce or
  1 tsp chili sambal
  (page 61)
salt and freshly ground black
  pepper

❶ Slice the plantain very thinly into rings. Put the oil in a heavy-based saucepan and heat until a cube of bread browns in seconds. Deep-fry the plantain slices in the hot oil for 3 minutes until crisp and golden. Drain well on paper towels.

❷ Whisk together the dressing ingredients and season to taste.

❸ Toss together the plantain chips, tomatoes, mango, scallions, and dressing. Serve immediately.

PIRI-PIRI

Not only is piri-piri very popular for seasoning casseroles in Portugal, it is also a much-used condiment in parts of southern Africa. It is used sparingly at the table to bring a little heat and flavor to plainer dishes.

SERVES 8

12 red chilies, seeded and finely chopped
½ cup vegetable oil
1 tsp finely chopped fresh oregano

freshly squeezed juice of 1 lemon
salt and freshly ground black pepper

❶ Pound the chilies in a mortar and pestle to make a paste. Gradually whisk in the oil, oregano, lemon juice, and salt to taste to make a smooth sauce.
❷ Store, covered, in the refrigerator for 3 to 5 days.

CHILI SAMBAL

Originating in Ghana, chili sambal is traditionally used to pep up plain rice and vegetable dishes. Spread it sparingly on cuts of fish or meat before char-grilling, or stir a little into simple sauces for extra flavor. It will keep in the refrigerator, covered, for up to 5 days.

SERVES 8

6 hot red chilies, seeded and roughly chopped
1 onion, roughly chopped
3 tomatoes, peeled, seeded, and roughly chopped
1 tbsp finely grated fresh gingerroot

1 tbsp vegetable oil
grated peel and freshly squeezed juice of 1 lime
salt and freshly ground black pepper

Place all the ingredients in a blender or food processor and whiz together until smooth.

GREEN PEPPER KETCHUP

This mildly hot, herby sauce is delicious splashed on to roasted meat and poultry. It will keep for at least 6 months if sealed and stored correctly.

MAKES ABOUT 3¾ CUPS

8 green bell peppers, seeded and diced
8 green chilies, seeded and halved
1 onion, roughly chopped
2 garlic cloves
2 slices fresh gingerroot
4½ cups malt vinegar
2–2¼ cups soft brown sugar
1 tbsp black peppercorns
1 tsp salt

❶ Place the peppers, chilies, onion, garlic, ginger, vinegar, and sugar to taste in a large saucepan.
❷ Bring to a boil, stirring until the sugar dissolves. Cover, lower the heat, and simmer very slowly, stirring occasionally for 1½ hours. Strain the mixture through a fine nonmetallic strainer, then pour immediately into hot, sterilized bottles. Seal (page 10) and store.

Hot Ginger Salsa

This sweet-and-sour, hot salsa is particularly good served with fried salt fish. It will only keep in the refrigerator for 1 to 2 hours before the flavors and colors fade, so be sure to eat it soon after it is made.

SERVES 2

3-inch piece fresh gingerroot
1 ripe papaya, peeled and roughly diced
2 garlic cloves, finely chopped

2 fresh red chilies, seeded and finely chopped
freshly squeezed juice of 1 lemon
salt and freshly ground black pepper

❶ Peel the ginger and grate it very finely. Place the papaya flesh in a bowl and mash it smooth with a fork.
❷ Stir in the ginger, garlic, chilies, lemon juice, and seasoning to taste. Cover and chill until needed.

Lime Sauce

This stimulating sauce is delicious added to peanut oil and tossed with a crisp green salad or sprinkled over plainly steamed or broiled seafood.

SERVES 4

2 garlic cloves
4 green chilies, seeded
3 tbsp fresh cilantro leaves
2 tbsp light soy sauce

3 tbsp sugar
freshly squeezed juice of 1 lime

Place the garlic, chilies, cilantro, and soy sauce in a blender or food processor and whiz until smooth. Add the sugar and about 6 tbsp water, stirring until the sugar dissolves. Stir in the lime juice and chill until required.

ASIA

THE PREDOMINANT CHARACTERISTIC OF Asian food is pungent, strong flavors imparted by aromatic spices, especially ginger. Alongside the spices, other flavors also feature, particularly chili, lemongrass, soy sauce, fish sauces, and shrimp paste. For the majority of the peasant population, the main source of protein in their diet is salted and dried fish, from which the powerful salty sauces and pastes that are used to flavor ketchups and salsas are derived.

Natural sugars from coconut paired with vinegar and sharp citrus and sour fruits, such as tamarind, give food the typical Asian sweet-and-sour taste, and salty sauces combined with hot chilies create another flavor typical of the region.

ASIAN INGREDIENTS

The floating market in Bangkok offers a wealth of fresh fruit and vegetables.

BASIL

A key ingredient in Thai and Vietnamese cooking, basil is a member of the mint family and appears in a number of different varieties, the most popular of which is the green "sweet" basil, readily available in most western countries. Purple, or opal, basil has a mild flavor that intensifies on cooking; it is difficult to find outside of Asia but can be easily grown in a window box.

CHILIES

The general rule with chilies is that the smaller and thinner skinned the chili is, the hotter it will be. Unlike the mild, thick-skinned Mexican jalapeño pepper, familiar in the West, Asian chilies are small, pointy, and packed with seeds. I advise you to shake out all of the seeds before adding chopped chilies to any dish, for however fiery you like your food, the seeds are very powerful, much more so than most people are used to. These types of chilies can be bought from Asian grocers, but you must take care when handling them as they can severely irritate the skin. If you have sensitive skin, wear rubber gloves while you seed and chop the chilies.

LEMONGRASS

This thick, almost woody grass is used throughout Southeast Asia to impart a subtle lemon flavor to soups, stocks, and curries. It is available fresh from specialist grocers and large supermarkets, and can be kept, loosely wrapped, in the refrigerator for up to 10 days.

FISH SAUCE

Strong and salty fish sauce is made in much the same way as soy sauce (see below). The liquid that is filtered off after fish and salt have been left to ferment is the thin, dark brown sauce that plays such an important role in the cuisines of Thailand, Vietnam, and Burma. In fact, it is served as a condiment with most meals in Vietnam, and with the addition of a little ground chili, ground nuts, or sugar makes a super dipping sauce.

GINGER

One of the most popular spices in Asian cooking, ginger is used fresh or pickled. When fresh, the root is peeled and thinly sliced or grated for inclusion in soups, stir-fries, ketchups, and sauces. In China and Japan, however, young roots are thinly sliced and pickled in vinegar. During the process a chemical reaction turns the ginger a delicate shade of pink, and it is often served as garnish to dishes such as sushi. You can find pickled ginger in Oriental supermarkets.

Bunches of chilies hung from a wall to dry naturally in the sun.

SHRIMP PASTE

Shrimp paste is made by pulverizing salted tiny shrimp. The paste is then compressed and dried into blocks that are stored in oil to avoid the strong odors that naturally accompany it.

SOY SAUCE

A sweet, salty sauce, soy sauce has been used in China for thousands of years. Made from fermented soybeans and roasted grains (usually wheat, but occasionally barley), it is left to mature in wooden casks for a number of months before being filtered and bottled. It is a vital ingredient in Chinese and Japanese cooking, and is also used as a condiment at the table. There are a great number of different soy sauces, including low- and reduced-sodium soy sauces, tamari, *and* shoyu.

JAPANESE GRAPEFRUIT SALSA

This refreshing salsa is a real palate-cleanser, and is wonderful served after a hot or spicy dish.

SERVES 4

2 grapefruit, peeled and
   segmented
1 cup fresh raspberries
1 tsp black peppercorns

½ cup sake
handful fresh basil leaves,
   shredded
¼ tsp salt

❶ Cut each grapefruit segment into 3 even, bite-size pieces, then place in serving bowl with the raspberries.
❷ Lightly pound the peppercorns in a mortar and pestle, then transfer to a small bowl. Stir in the sake, basil, and salt and pour the dressing over the grapefruit salsa. Toss together. Cover and chill for 1 hour before serving.

RED PEPPER SAMBAL

This spicy sambal is very popular in Indonesia, where it is served on the side with almost every meal. Keep it in a screw-top jar in the refrigerator for up to a week.

MAKES ABOUT 1 CUP

1 large red bell pepper,
   weighing about 8 ounces,
   seeded and roughly chopped
1 tsp shrimp paste
1 tsp chili flakes

4 tbsp sunflower oil
1 tsp dark brown sugar
½ tsp salt
freshly squeezed juice of 1 lime

❶ Whiz the pepper, shrimp paste, and chili flakes together in a food processor until smooth and well blended.
❷ Heat the sunflower oil in a wok or skillet and stir-fry the pepper mixture for about 5 minutes, until it becomes dark red and the oil separates. Add the sugar and salt and stir until the sugar dissolves.
❸ Stir in the lime juice and remove the pan from the heat. Leave the sambal to cool, then cover and chill until ready to use.

Japanese Grapefruit Salsa

SPICY THAI SALSA

This salsa is very potent, so only a small amount is needed.

SERVES 6

6 shallots, halved
6 garlic cloves
6 green chilies
1 tbsp sunflower oil
1 large tomato, seeded and cut
    into tiny dice

1 tsp shrimp paste
1 tbsp fish sauce
2 tbsp freshly squeezed lime
    juice
salt and freshly ground black
    pepper

❶ Preheat the broiler to high. Brush the shallots, garlic, and green chilies with the oil, then place under the broiler for 8 minutes, turning them over once, until tender and a little charred. Roughly chop the shallots and garlic and place in a serving bowl.

❷ Carefully cut open the chilies and shake out and discard the seeds. Finely chop the chili flesh and set aside.

❸ Stir the tomato dice into the shallot mixture. Whisk together the shrimp paste, fish sauce, lime juice, and chopped chili. Spoon the mixture over the vegetables and toss together. Check the seasoning and serve warm or at room temperature.

SATAY SAUCE

Satay sauce is traditionally served with skewered meat and chicken, but I also find a heaped tablespoonful makes a welcome addition to vegetable stir-fries. Bars of creamed coconut are sold at Asian and Chinese grocery stores.

SERVES 4

2 ounces creamed coconut
3 tbsp smooth peanut butter
1 tbsp soy sauce
2 tbsp freshly squeezed lemon
 juice

1 tbsp raw peanuts, peeled and
 roughly chopped
salt and freshly ground black
 pepper

❶ Heat the creamed coconut with the peanut butter, soy sauce, and lemon juice in a small saucepan. Gradually whisk in ⅔ cup boiling water to make a smooth, thick sauce.
❷ Dry-fry the peanuts in a nonstick skillet for 2 to 4 minutes until golden; stir into the sauce. Season and serve warm.

JAPANESE SAKE SAUCE

Brush this sweet glazing sauce onto chicken or fish about halfway through roasting to give a sweet and salty, crisp, shiny coat.

MAKES ABOUT 1¼ CUPS

⅔ cup shoyu sauce
6 tbsp sugar

⅔ cup sake (Japanese rice wine)

❶ Place the shoyu sauce, sugar, and sake in a small saucepan and bring to a boil. Lower the heat and simmer slowly, stirring occasionally, for 5 minutes, until the sauce turns slightly syrupy.
❷ Use immediately, or allow to cool and use as a marinade for fish or tofu.

Hot-*and*-Sour Salsa

This piquant salsa is made with white radish–look out for it in the stores labeled as mooli or daikon.
For an authentic Japanese touch, peel the broccoli stem, slice it thickly on the diagonal, and add to the salsa along with the flowerets.

SERVES 6

1 head broccoli, head cut into tiny flowerets and stem sliced (see above)
2 carrots, cut into sticks
1 small white radish, peeled and diced

FOR THE DRESSING
3 small red chilies, seeded and finely chopped
1 garlic clove
2 tbsp soy sauce
freshly squeezed juice of 1 lemon
1 tsp sugar
salt

❶ Place the broccoli flowerets and stem slices, if adding, carrot sticks, and radish cubes in a serving bowl.
❷ To make the dressing, pound the chilies and garlic together in a mortar and pestle to form a paste. Stir in the soy sauce, lemon juice, sugar, and salt to taste.
❸ Add the dressing to the bowl and toss the salsa together well. Cover and chill for 2 hours before serving.

Long Bean Salsa

If you cannot get hold of long beans, thin French-style green beans will do. Long beans are sold at Oriental grocery stores.

SERVES 4

bunch long beans, weighing about 4 ounces
1 tbsp sesame seeds
6 slices pickled ginger, finely shredded

2 tbsp light soy sauce
2 tbsp freshly squeezed lemon juice
salt

❶ Trim the beans and cut into lengths about 1 inch long. Plunge into a pan of boiling salted water for exactly 1 minute. Drain and cool completely under cold running water. Drain well again and place in a bowl.
❷ Place the sesame seeds in a nonstick skillet and dry-roast for 1 to 2 minutes, until golden. Add to the bowl of beans with the pickled ginger, soy sauce, lemon juice, and salt to taste.
❸ Toss the salsa together. Cover and chill for 1 to 2 hours or until ready to serve.

Hot and Sour Salsa

CUCUMBER *AND* CARROT ACAR

An *acar* is an Asian salsa made from vegetables tossed with vinegar and spices. This fresh-tasting Thai *acar*, with its clean taste, is a good accompaniment to rich fish and meat dishes. Keep it covered, in the refrigerator, for up to 2 days.

SERVES 4 TO 6

1 cucumber	*1 tbsp chopped scallion*
1 carrot, cut into tiny dice	*2 tbsp fish sauce*
3 small Asian chilies, seeded	*2 tbsp white vinegar*
and finely chopped	*1 tbsp sugar*

❶ Peel the cucumber and cut it in half lengthwise. Using a teaspoon, scoop out and discard the seeds.
❷ Thinly slice the cucumber into half-moon shapes, then place them in a bowl with the remaining ingredients.
❸ Toss together. Serve immediately or cover and chill for use later.

CURRIED CAULIFLOWER SALSA

This Indian-style salsa makes a delicious appetizer or accompaniment served with crispy poppadums and red-onion raita. If using frozen peas in place of fresh, add them in step 2 with the lemon juice.

SERVES 4

1 tbsp vegetable oil	*2 ripe tomatoes, roughly*
1 onion, finely chopped	*chopped*
2 garlic cloves, finely chopped	*⅓ cup peas*
1 tsp cumin seeds	*juice of 1 lemon*
1 red chili, seeded and finely	*1 tsp turmeric*
chopped	*2 tbsp chopped fresh cilantro*
1⅓ cups small cauliflower	*salt and freshly ground black*
flowerets	*pepper*

❶ Heat the oil in a wok or large skillet. Add the onion, garlic, cumin, chili, cauliflower, tomatoes, and peas and stir-fry for 5 minutes, adding a little more oil or 1 tbsp of the lemon juice if the mixture is too dry.
❷ Stir in the turmeric and lemon juice and season to taste. Cook for 2 minutes longer, then stir in the cilantro. Serve immediately or let cool and reheat to serve.

RED-ONION RAITA To make red onion raita, stir a small finely chopped red onion and a handful of chopped mint into a pot of plain yogurt. Season with salt to taste.

Cucumber and Carrot Acar

THAI TOMATO SAUCE

This mouthwatering tomato sauce makes a super accompaniment to fried appetizers and nibbles, such as rolls or crab cakes. Keep any leftover sauce, covered, in the refrigerator for 2 to 3 days.

SERVES 6

3 cups peeled, seeded, and
   roughly chopped tomatoes
1 tbsp sunflower oil
2 tsp sesame oil
1 tbsp tamarind paste (see
   right)

handful fresh basil leaves
1 stalk fresh lemongrass
2 tbsp dark soy sauce
1 tsp hot chili sauce
salt and freshly ground black
   pepper

❶ Place all the ingredients in a saucepan, cover, and simmer slowly, stirring occasionally, for 45 minutes until thick and pulpy.
❷ Strain the sauce through a fine nonmetallic strainer, then return to the rinsed-out pan. Season to taste and heat through. Serve hot.

TAMARIND PASTE

To make tamarind paste, beat 1 heaped tbsp of standard tamarind pulp with 3 tbsp boiling water. Pass the mixture through a fine nonmetallic strainer to make a smooth, very thick sauce. Store in the refrigerator for up to a week. You can buy tamarind paste at Oriental supermarkets.

ALL-PURPOSE DIPPING SAUCE

This incredibly versatile dipping sauce can be
served with any number of dishes. Try it with fried or
steamed cubes of tofu or strips of broiled meat.

SERVES 4

*4 tbsp shoyu or other high-
quality soy sauce*
2 tbsp white-wine vinegar

1 tbsp sesame oil
1 tsp dark brown sugar
1 tsp chili flakes

Blend all the ingredients together with 1 tbsp water.

Variations Add any one or a combination of the following for
a good variation of the All-Purpose Dipping Sauce:

chopped fresh cilantro or basil
toasted sesame seeds
finely diced tomato
crushed garlic clove

grated cucumber
finely chopped fresh green chili
finely chopped scallion

CARIBBEAN

THE STORMY, TROPICAL CLIMATE *of the Caribbean islands produces a wealth of exotic fruit and vegetables, which, combined with aromatic herbs and spices, produce a distinctive cuisine. Gathering influences from many different sources, including Africa and Europe, Caribbean food is fresh and exciting. It uses a mélange of traditional and historical methods of cooking and is continually absorbing new combinations of flavors.*

A fundamental aspect of family eating is the buffet with many dishes served together on one table—you will find plainer rice, bean, and cornmeal dishes enlivened by bowls of vibrant salsas and colorful ketchups. And many typical dishes, such as Jamaican jerk chicken, involve marinating and brushing meat, fish, or poultry with fresh herbs and spices, establishing a regular use for the flavorsome ketchups and sauces.

CARIBBEAN INGREDIENTS

BANANA

Sweet, ripe bananas are an essential ingredient in tropical food. They are at their best when deep yellow with just a few, if any, black spots. Don't choose soft bananas with black peels. If using them raw, squeeze a little fresh lemon or lime juice over the cut surfaces to help prevent browning.

COCONUT

Fresh coconuts are readily available from grocery stores on the islands. When choosing yours, shake it to make sure it has plenty of juice inside–a good sign of freshness. Crack the shell and shake out all the liquid, then peel off the papery skin and dice, grate, shave, or chop the flesh. To make coconut

Plump purple eggplants and orange-fleshed squashes are examples of the region's colorful and distinctive ingredients.

milk, chop the flesh and place it in a bowl, then cover with boiling water and leave to cool completely. Strain the liquid through cheesecloth, then it is ready to use in a whole host of dishes, such as soups, curries, and drinks to name just a few. At Caribbean and Asian grocers, you can also buy creamed coconut in blocks which can be crumbled into a dish; dried shredded coconut can be used to make coconut milk in the same way as fresh. Rich in protein, vitamins, and oil, coconut has a high nutritional value. However, unlike nut and vegetable oils, coconut oil is a saturated fat with a high cholesterol content, so it should be eaten sparingly.

Lemon

The sharp tang of lemons makes them unsuitable to eat as a fruit, but they are used to flavor inummerable sweet and savory dishes, as well as in baking and for making marmalades, chutneys, and ketchups. Lemon juice also helps to prevent the natural discoloration (enzymic browning) of certain fruits, such as pear and avocado, when the cut surface is exposed to the air–this is particularly useful to remember if you are planning to prepare fruit in advance of serving.

Mango

Originally from Asia, the mango is now closely associated with Caribbean food. It is not really possible to judge the ripeness of a mango by the color of its skin, as some are ripe even when green. To test for ripeness, squeeze the flesh gently and it should give slightly; do not choose mangoes that are hard or have wrinkled or black, blotchy skins. Take care that your knife doesn't slip when you slice the flesh from the large, flat, slippery seed before peeling and dicing the sweet flesh. Use raw in desserts or cooked in hot salsas and ketchups.

MELON SALSA

This sweet-and-sour salsa uses a
blend of white rum, light brown sugar, and fresh lemon
juice to give a tropical taste of the Caribbean.

SERVES 4

*1 small sweet melon, such as
   Persian or Galia, peeled,
   seeded, and diced*
4 tbsp white rum
1 small red onion, finely diced
*1 green chili, seeded and finely
   chopped*

2 tbsp fresh cilantro
1 tsp light brown sugar
*freshly squeezed juice of ½
   lemon*
*salt and freshly ground black
   pepper*

❶ Place the melon and rum in a large bowl. Cover and chill
for 1 to 2 hours, stirring gently once or twice.
❷ When ready to serve, stir in the onion, chili, cilantro,
sugar, lemon juice, and seasoning to taste.

TROPICAL SALSA

Serve this sunny salsa as part of a meal or,
if planning a dinner party, this quantity will serve 4
as a light first course.

SERVES 4

1 large ripe papaya, diced
1 large ripe avocado, diced
*2 thick slices fresh pineapple,
   cored and diced*
2 tbsp soy sauce
*grated peel and freshly squeezed
   juice of 1 orange*
2 tbsp peanut oil

2 tbsp dark brown sugar
1 garlic clove, finely chopped
*½-inch piece fresh gingerroot,
   finely grated*
½ tsp chili flakes
4 tbsp chopped fresh cilantro
4 tbsp chopped fresh mint
*salt and freshly ground black
   pepper*

❶ Place the papaya, avocado, and pineapple in a large bowl.
❷ Mix together the soy sauce, orange juice, oil, and sugar,
stirring until the sugar dissolves. Whisk in the garlic, ginger,
chili flakes, orange peel, cilantro, and mint, then season to
taste.
❸ Pour the dressing over the fruit and toss together. Cover
and chill for 1 to 2 hours before serving.

Melon Salsa

JAMAICAN JERK SAUCE

Throughout the Caribbean, jerk sauce is rubbed onto meat before it is barbecued or broiled. Jerk seasonings and sauces always contain a special combination of spices which includes cinnamon, nutmeg, and allspice. If you prefer a slightly more pungent sauce, don't broil the scallions but add them raw.

SERVES 6

6 scallions
4 tbsp roughly chopped fresh
   thyme
4 garlic cloves, roughly chopped
½-inch piece fresh gingerroot,
   roughly chopped
3 red chilies, seeded and finely
   chopped

½ tsp grated nutmeg
¼ tsp ground cinnamon
1 tsp ground allspice
4 tbsp soy sauce
2 tbsp white vinegar
salt and freshly ground black
   pepper

❶ Preheat the broiler. Broil the scallions for 5 minutes, turning them once, until tender and a little charred. Chop finely.
❷ Pound together the thyme, garlic, ginger, and chilies in a mortar and pestle to form a paste. Pound in the chopped scallions.
❸ Stir in the ground spices, soy sauce, white vinegar, and seasoning to taste.

LEMON *AND* LIME KETCHUP

This ketchup takes six months to mature before it's ready to serve, but the tangy citrus flavor is excellent for salad dressings, marinades, and soups, so it's worth the wait.

MAKES ABOUT 5 CUPS
4 lemons
4 limes
6 tbsp salt
1 onion, finely chopped
2 garlic cloves, finely chopped
3¾ cups white-wine vinegar

1 tsp whole cloves, lightly crushed
1 tbsp ground ginger
1 tsp whole black peppercorns, lightly crushed

❶ Peel the lemons and limes and slice them thickly. Rub the salt into the flesh and layer them in hot, sterilized jars with the onion and garlic.

❷ Place the vinegar, cloves, ginger, and peppercorns in a saucepan and bring to a boil. Pour over the lemons, seal with vinegar-proof lids, and store for 6 months.

❸ Strain the ketchup into sterilized bottles. Seal (page 10) and store for up to 12 months.

PASSIONATE SALSA

Serve this fruity salsa with hot
crêpes, or yogurt for a flavorsome dessert or weekend
breakfast. Serve chilled.

SERVES 4

4 pomegranates
4 passion fruit
1-inch piece candied
    ginger in syrup
2 tbsp syrup from the jar
    of ginger

freshly squeezed juice of 1 lime
1 tbsp peanut oil
1 tsp whole black peppercorns,
    lightly crushed
1 tsp brown sugar
1 tbsp chopped fresh mint
¼ tsp kosher salt

❶ Cut the pomegranates and passion fruit in half and scoop
out the flesh and seeds into a bowl.
❷ Finely chop the candied ginger and mix with the ginger
syrup, lime juice, and peanut oil. Spoon over the fruit and
mix together. Cover and chill until ready to serve.
❸ When ready to serve, divide the salsa into individual
serving dishes and sprinkle with the pepper, sugar, mint,
and salt.

PEACH *AND* RAISIN SALSA

Add a touch of spice to this peachy salsa by stirring
in ½ tsp of ground cinnamon at step 3.

SERVES 4

8 peaches, halved and pitted
2 tbsp vegetable oil
1 large onion, finely chopped
1-inch piece fresh gingerroot,
   finely grated
heaped 1 cup soft brown sugar
½ cup raisins

½ cup freshly squeezed orange
   juice
½ cup red-wine vinegar
salt and freshly ground black
   pepper

❶ Preheat the broiler to medium hot. Lightly brush the
peaches with oil and place under the broiler for 15 minutes,
turning once, until tender and golden.
❷ Meanwhile, heat the remaining oil in a small saucepan.
Add the onion and ginger and cook slowly, stirring occasionally, for 5 minutes, until softened.
❸ Cut the peaches into small pieces and add to the pan
with the sugar, raisins, orange juice, and vinegar. Bring to a
boil, then cover, lower the heat, and simmer for 40 minutes.
❹ Season to taste and allow to cool completely. Store in the
refrigerator, covered, for up to 10 days.

PINEAPPLE SALSA

This fruity Caribbean salsa tastes super with broiled chicken and fried salt-cod fish cakes. It can be kept, covered, in the refrigerator for up to 2 days.

SERVES 4 TO 6

heaped 1 cup peeled and cored pineapple cut into small dice
2 tbsp chopped fresh cilantro
grated peel and freshly squeezed juice of ½ lime

½-inch piece fresh gingerroot, finely grated
1 tsp light brown sugar
salt and freshly ground black pepper

❶ Place the pineapple, cilantro, lime juice and peel, and ginger in a large bowl and toss together.
❷ Stir in the sugar and season to taste with salt and pepper.
❸ Cover and chill in the refrigerator for at least 2 hours until ready to serve.

PAN-FRIED FRUIT SALSA

Turn this savory salsa into a sweet one by omitting the garlic and chili and adding a tablespoon or two of honey in place of the hot-pepper sauce.

SERVES 4

1 tsp vegetable oil
1 garlic clove, thinly sliced
1 red chili, seeded and thinly sliced
2 thick slices fresh pineapple, cut into chunks

2 green mangoes, cubed
4 tbsp fresh pineapple juice
few drops hot-pepper sauce
salt and freshly ground black pepper

❶ Heat the oil in a wok or large skillet and stir-fry the garlic, chili, pineapple, and mango over high heat for 5 minutes until golden brown.
❷ Add the pineapple juice and hot-pepper sauce and heat through for 2 minutes until piping hot. Season to taste and serve immediately.

Sweet Potato
and Coconut Salsa

For a simple and tasty tropical supper, brush 4 small fish, such as red snapper, with a little oil and roast in the oven with the salsa for the final 20 minutes. Serve the fish with the salsa and some crisp green salad on the side.

SERVES 4

3 cups cubed sweet potatoes
2 tbsp vegetable oil
14-ounce can pineapple chunks
  in natural juice, drained
2 cups thick coconut milk
freshly squeezed juice of
  ½ lemon

1 red chili, seeded and finely
  chopped
salt and freshly ground black
  pepper

❶ Preheat the oven to 400°F. Place the sweet potato in a roasting pan and drizzle the oil and a little seasoning over. Roast in the oven for 20 minutes.
❷ Stir in the pineapple chunks, coconut milk, lemon juice, chili, and seasoning. Return to the oven and roast for 20 minutes longer, until the potatoes are tender and the salsa has thickened.

BANANA *AND* GINGER KETCHUP

This tropical ketchup is perfect
to serve with grilled or broiled chicken and fish,
or with a platter of sharp-tasting cheese.

MAKES ABOUT 3¾ CUPS

*10 ripe bananas, peeled and
roughly chopped*
2 onions, finely chopped
*2-inch piece gingerroot, finely
grated*

2½ cups cider vinegar
2 cups soft brown sugar
2 tsp black peppercorns
1 tsp allspice berries
1 tsp salt

❶ Place the bananas, onions, ginger, vinegar, sugar, spices, and salt in a large saucepan. Bring to a boil, stirring until the sugar dissolves. Cover and simmer gently for 1 hour, stirring occasionally, until thick and pulpy.

❷ Strain the mixture through a fine nonmetallic strainer, then pour immediately into hot, sterilized bottles. Seal (page 10) and store for up to 6 months.

Hot Mango Salsa

Serve this fiery salsa with a bowl
of tortilla chips for an irresistible party dip.

SERVES 4

1 tbsp vegetable oil
1 large onion, finely chopped
2 green chilies, seeded and
 finely chopped
2 ripe mangoes, peeled and
 diced

2 ripe tomatoes, diced
freshly squeezed juice of 2 limes
1 tbsp soft brown sugar
salt and freshly ground black
 pepper

❶ Heat the oil in a small saucepan and gently cook the onion and chilies for 5 minutes until softened.
❷ Add the mangoes and tomatoes, cover, and cook very slowly for 30 minutes.
❸ Stir in the lime juice and sugar and season to taste, adding more sugar if necessary. Serve hot or cold.

SOUTH AMERICA

As well as covering *South America*, this chapter also includes *Mexico* – the home of the salsa. For that reason, there are only salsa recipes here, many of which are classical dishes that you may have tried before. Serve these salsas with sizzling chicken or shrimp fajitas, and as tastebud-tickling dipping sauces for fiery tortilla chips, crispy tacos, and cheese nachos.

The two most valuable ingredients of this culinary region are corn, which is used to make, among many other things, the essential tortilla, and chilies, which are the most crucial component of almost all salsas.

SOUTH AMERICAN *and* MEXICAN INGREDIENTS

Giant scallions and fresh limes on a Mexican market.

JALAPEÑO

The jalapeño *chili pepper is a very popular ingredient in both raw and cooked salsas. It is relatively large and plump with dark green, thick flesh that is medium hot. When dried, the jalapeño turns a rusty brown color and is then known as a* chipotle *chili.*

PEQUIN

This tiny, dark red chili is extremely fiery. Usually only available dried whole or in flakes, it should be used sparingly in sauces or added to flasks of oil to make chili oil. Never attempt to eat a whole pequin.

POBLANO

This large chili and the pasilla *are very similar. It is mild to medium-hot with a rich, distinctive flavor. It is also popular dried, when it becomes* very wrinkled and acquires a smoky taste. Dried poblanoes *may be dark red, when they are known as* ancho, *or dark brown and known as* mulato.

In Mexico, the home of salsa, there's no shortage of fresh and flavorsome produce.

SUNSHINE SALSA

This beautiful salsa really does
bring a ray of sunshine to the dining table. Serve as a
refreshing accompaniment to fish.

SERVES 4

2 yellow tomatoes, thinly sliced

2 ripe red tomatoes, thinly
sliced

2 small oranges, peeled, and
thinly sliced into rounds

1 tsp bottled pink peppercorns,
lightly crushed

1 garlic clove, finely chopped

2 tbsp chopped fresh parsley,
coriander or chives

2 tbsp extra-virgin olive oil

salt and freshly ground black
pepper

❶ Arrange the tomatoes and orange slices on a large round
serving platter.
❷ Whisk together the peppercorns, garlic, herbs, olive oil
and plenty of seasoning. Drizzle over the salsa and serve
immediately.

CHIMICHURRI

This is a South American classic. Popular in Argentina and Brazil, chimichurri is a simple salsa based on onions, parsley, and chili. It is traditionally served with plain broiled or barbecued meats.

SERVES 6

2 red onions or 4 purple shallots, finely chopped
2 hot red chilies, seeded and finely chopped
1 large garlic clove, finely chopped

4 tbsp chopped fresh parsley
2 tbsp olive oil
freshly squeezed juice of 1 lemon
salt and freshly ground black pepper

Place all the ingredients in a large bowl and toss together well. Season to taste, cover, and chill for 1 to 2 hours before serving.

SALSA VERDE

This and *salsa cruda* (page 105) are examples of the many green salsas enjoyed in South America. The ingredients are traditionally chopped by hand, but if you prefer a smoother salsa, whiz them in a mini food processor or blender.

SERVES 6

6 scallions, finely chopped
1 onion, finely chopped
2 garlic cloves, finely chopped
2 green chilies, seeded and
  finely chopped
6 tbsp chopped fresh cilantro
6 tbsp chopped fresh flat-leaf
  parsley
1 tbsp capers, well drained and
  finely chopped (optional)
4 tbsp olive oil
freshly squeezed juice and
  grated peel of 1 lemon
salt and freshly ground black
  pepper

Place all the ingredients in a large serving bowl and toss together. Season to taste and serve immediately.

HOT GUACAMOLE

Like all South American salsas, this one makes a brilliant dipping sauce for nachos and tortilla chips.

SERVES 4

2 garlic cloves, roughly chopped
2 red chilies, seeded and
  roughly chopped
6 black peppercorns
2 large avocados
2 tbsp olive oil
juice of 1 lemon
salt

❶ Pound the garlic, chilies, and peppercorns in a mortar and pestle to make a paste.
❷ Peel and seed the avocados, then mash the flesh well. Stir in the chili paste, olive oil, and lemon juice. Season to taste, cover and refrigerate until ready to serve.

PICO DE GALLO

There are many versions of this
Mexican salsa, whose title translates as "rooster's beak."
Here's my version, which is best spooned onto cheese-
covered tacos and burritos or drizzled over
sizzling chicken or beef.

SERVES 6

4 tomatoes, roughly chopped
1 red onion, finely chopped
10 radishes, roughly chopped
2 green chilies, seeded and
 finely chopped

2 tbsp chopped fresh cilantro
freshly squeezed juice of 1 lime
¼ tsp salt

Place all the ingredients in a large bowl and toss together.
Serve immediately.

SALSA CON QUESO

This dish is always on the menu in Mexican-style restaurants and simply needs tortillas or tacos to make a complete snack-meal for two.

SERVES 2

1 tbsp vegetable oil
1 small onion, finely chopped
2 garlic cloves, finely chopped
4 slices bacon, roughly chopped
14-ounce can crushed plum
    tomatoes

2 tsp chili flakes
½ tsp salt
1 cup grated full-flavored
    cheese, such as sharp
    cheddar or Monterey jack
    grated

❶ Heat the oil in a pan and slowly cook the onion, garlic, and bacon for about 5 minutes, stirring occasionally, until tender and golden. Add the can of tomatoes, chili flakes, and salt and bring to a boil, then cover and simmer for 15 minutes.
❷ Meanwhile, preheat the broiler.
❸ Transfer the mixture to a shallow flameproof dish and scatter the cheese over. Place under the broiler for about 5 minutes until bubbling and golden. Serve immediately.

SALSA CRUDA

There are endless raw South American
salsas, all going under the name of *salsa cruda*; this is
a very simple version that is delicious scooped
up with tortilla chips for a snack
or served as part of a meal.

SERVES 4

*2 large tomatoes, roughly
    chopped*
8 scallions, roughly chopped
*2 hot green chilies, seeded and
    finely chopped*
*2 tbsp chopped fresh parsley or
    cilantro*

*freshly squeezed juice of ½
    lemon*
1 tbsp olive oil
*salt and freshly ground black
    pepper*

Place all the ingredients in a large bowl and toss together.
Season to taste, cover, and chill for at least 2 hours before
serving.

ROASTED HABANERO SALSA

Habanero, or Scotch Bonnets, are one of
the hottest chili peppers. Unlike other fiery chilies,
they're not just hot but they are flavorsome, too.
Mix a little of this salsa with plain pasta or rice.

SERVES 4

6 ripe plum tomatoes, halved
5 tbsp extra-virgin olive oil
4 garlic cloves, crushed
10 habanero chili peppers
1 red onion, finely chopped

freshly squeezed juice of 1
  lemon
2 tbsp chopped fresh cilantro
salt and freshly ground black
  pepper

❶ Preheat the oven to 475°F. Arrange the tomatoes, cut side
up, on a baking sheet and drizzle with 1 tbsp olive oil.
Sprinkle with a little garlic, salt, and black pepper, then
roast for 15 minutes, until beginning to char.
❷ Meanwhile, skewer the chilies with a fork and hold them
one at a time on the flame of a gas ring for about 3 minutes,
until blistered. When they are all blistered, slip off the skins
and chop the flesh finely. If you don't have gas, place the
chilies under a hot broiler for 5 to 6 minutes, turning once.
❸ Dice the tomatoes and place them in a bowl with the
chopped chilies, remaining olive oil and garlic, red onion,
lemon juice, cilantro, and a little seasoning. Keep covered in
the refrigerator for up to 5 days, or until required.

SALSA CALIENTE

This sauce is the base of many dishes such as Oaxacan Eggs, a specialty of the Mexican state of Oaxaca. There eggs are poached in *salsa caliente* and sprinkled with grated cheese before serving. If you find the sauce too thick, stir in a little hot chicken or vegetable stock. This also makes a very good accompaniment to most meat and fish, and it can be served as a dip.

SERVES 4

4 large ripe tomatoes, halved
   and seeded
2 tbsp vegetable oil
2 jalapeño chilies, seeded and
   finely chopped
2 garlic cloves, finely chopped

1 small onion, finely chopped
chicken or vegetable stock,
   optional
salt and freshly ground black
   pepper

❶ Preheat the broiler. Brush the tomato halves with a little oil and broil for about 8 minutes, turning them once, until softened and a little charred. Peel and discard the skins and chop the flesh roughly.

❷ Meanwhile, pound the chilies, garlic, and onion using a mortar and pestle until they form a fairly smooth paste.

❸ Heat the remaining oil in a small skillet and cook the paste and tomatoes slowly for about 5 minutes until thick and pulpy, adding stock if necessary. Season to taste and serve hot, or cover and chill for up to 5 days. This salsa freezes well.

TOMATILLO SALSA

SWEET ONION SALSA

If you can find fresh tomatillos, remove the papery skins, halve the tomatillos, and simmer them gently in water until tender. This fruity salsa will keep, covered in the refrigerator, for up to 5 days.

SERVES 6

2 fresh papayas, peeled and diced
1 small onion, finely chopped
1 red bell pepper, seeded and diced
1 green bell pepper, seeded and diced
8-ounce can tomatillos, drained and finely chopped

1 small, hot red chili, seeded and finely chopped
2 tbsp chopped fresh cilantro
2 garlic cloves, finely chopped
freshly squeezed juice of 1 orange
2 tbsp olive oil
salt and freshly ground black pepper

❶ Place the papaya, onion, and peppers in a bowl.
❷ Mix together the tomatillos, chili, cilantro, garlic, orange juice, and olive oil and season well to taste. Add to the papaya mixture and toss together. Cover and chill until ready to serve.

The sautéeing process in this recipe turns the starches in the onions into sugar, hence a sweet, caramelized flavor. This salsa is delicious with tangy cheese and soft bread.

SERVES 4

2 tbsp vegetable oil
4 onions, thinly sliced
2 garlic cloves, finely chopped
2 tbsp chopped fresh parsley

1 tbsp freshly squeezed lemon juice
salt and freshly ground black pepper

❶ Heat the oil in a large skillet and slowly sauté the onions for 20 minutes, until soft and golden brown. Stir in the garlic and cook for 2 to 3 minutes longer.
❷ Transfer the mixture to a bowl and stir in the parsley and lemon juice. Season to taste and serve warm.

NORTH AMERICA

FROM THE SOPHISTICATED, MEDITERRANEAN -inspired cuisine of California to the traditional Deep South flavors of Louisiana, American food is plentiful and bursting with vitality. And, throughout the States, regional food is truly coming into its own -not only the flavor-packed and almost vegetarian style of cooking and eating from California. On the other side of the continent, Florida is undergoing a food revolution, too. There the Latin-American community is playing a major role in the state-wide trend towards the fusion of South American and Jamaican-influenced food.

North American Ingredients

Ripe tomatoes are the heart of classic ketchups and salsas.

Corn

Originally from Mexico, corn is an important ingredient in the United States. If eating it on the cob, the best way to cook it is to simply boil it for about 5 minutes, until the kernels are bright yellow and tender–do not salt the water because it toughens the kernels while they cook. Instead season after cooking and brush with melted butter.

Another delicious way to cook corn-on-the-cob is to sprinkle on a little fresh lime juice and barbecue it over hot coals, as I do in the recipe on page 118. If you want to remove the kernels, use a large, sharp knife to slice them off the cob.

Cranberries

Very tart when raw, cranberries are at their best when they are cooked, and they are great made into a ketchup, jam, or sauce. Used in place of raisins and dried berries, they are also delicious baked in muffins and fruit pies. They are mainly grown in Massachusetts and are harvested in winter, so look for them fresh in the stores from late October through to early February. Cranberries are extremely robust and store well when fresh but are also available frozen and dried, both of which make very good substitutes for the fresh.

RED ONIONS

Just one member of the enormous onion family, red onions, with their sweet and mild flavor, are particularly suitable for stirring raw into salsas. Their beautiful red/purple coloring also stands up to heat, making them a valuable addition to cooked ketchups and salsas, too.

TOMATILLOS

Also known as husk tomatoes and Mexican green tomatillos, these come wrapped in a papery skin that must be removed before you use the flesh. The sour flavor is a valuable ingredient in salsas throughout the United States and South America. In fact, tomatillos are often included in salsa verde. *They are available both fresh and canned.*

Whether boiled or barbecued, corn is a complement of many salsas.

ROASTED PEPPER SALSA

This Californian salsa is very much influenced by cooking from the Mediterranean. It is important that the peppers are left covered for 5 minutes after broiling because the gentle steam that results helps lift the skin away from the flesh.

SERVES 4

2 red bell peppers
2 yellow bell peppers
2 orange bell peppers
2 garlic cloves, finely chopped
2 ripe tomatoes, finely diced

2 tbsp chopped fresh flat-leaf
   parsley
4 tbsp extra-virgin olive oil
3 tbsp balsamic vinegar
salt and freshly ground black
   pepper

❶ Preheat the broiler to medium hot. Place all the peppers under the broiler for about 10 minutes, turning them frequently, until blackened and charred. Cover with a dish towel and leave to cool for 5 minutes.

❷ With the point of a sharp knife, pierce a hole in the bottom of each pepper and squeeze all the juice into a pitcher. Peel away the skin and discard, then cut the flesh into very thin ¼-inch thick slices.

❸ Place the warm pepper strips in a serving bowl with the garlic, tomatoes, and parsley. Whisk together the pepper juices, olive oil, and balsamic vinegar and season to taste. Pour over the peppers and toss together. Serve while still warm, or cover and chill for up to 4 days.

Classic American Tomato Ketchup

Serve this old-fashioned favorite with just about anything. Try topping cheese on toast with a spoonful of this rich, thick ketchup, or simply use it for dipping your fries into.

MAKES ABOUT 5 CUPS

3 pounds ripe tomatoes, quartered
2 garlic cloves, halved
½ cup cider vinegar
¼ cup sugar

½ tsp ground ginger
½ tsp salt
4 black peppercorns
4 cloves

❶ Place the tomatoes and garlic in a large saucepan. Cover and stew down very gently for 1 hour, stirring occasionally, until thick and pulpy.

❷ Purée the tomato pulp in a food processor or blender until smooth, then return it to the rinsed-out pan. Add the remaining vinegar, sugar, and spices. Bring to a boil, stirring, until the sugar dissolves. Cover and simmer for 45 minutes, stirring until thick and smooth.

❸ Strain the mixture through a fine nonmetallic strainer, then pour immediately into hot, sterilized bottles. Seal (page 10) and store until required.

SWEET CHERRY KETCHUP

Serve this seasonal ketchup with hamburgers, or as a dip for crispy fries or onion rings.

MAKES ABOUT 3¾ CUPS

1 onion, roughly chopped
2 large cooking apples, cored, peeled, and roughly chopped
2 pounds morello cherries, pitted
2 cups red-wine vinegar
2 to 2¼ cups soft brown sugar
½-inch piece gingerroot
½ tsp ground cinnamon
½ tsp salt

❶ Place all the ingredients in a large pan and bring to a boil, stirring until the sugar dissolves. Cover and simmer for 1 hour, stirring occasionally.
❷ Strain the mixture through a fine nonmetallic strainer, then pour immediately into hot, sterilized bottles. Seal (page 10) and store until required.

ROASTED CORN SALSA

Fill a baked potato with a spoonful
of sour cream and top with this fragrant salsa for a
super light lunch. Remember to choose the freshest,
juiciest corn cobs.

SERVES 8

4 corn cobs
freshly squeezed juice of 2 limes
4 tomatoes, seeded and finely
*   diced*
2 red onions, finely chopped

4 tbsp chopped fresh cilantro
3 tbsp olive oil
salt and freshly ground black
*   pepper*

❶ Brush the corn cobs with a little of the lime juice and
sprinkle with salt. Slowly barbecue or broil for 20 to 30 minutes, turning them over occasionally, until tender and
golden. Using a large, heavy knife, slice down the cobs to
remove the kernels.

❷ Place the corn kernels in a bowl with the tomatoes, red
onions, and cilantro. Whisk together the olive oil and remaining lime juice. Season to taste and pour over the salsa.
Toss well to mix and serve while still slightly warm, or leave
to cool, cover, and chill for up to 2 hours.

INSTANT TOMATO SALSA

This speedy salsa takes literally seconds to prepare and serve as a great dip for corn chips.

SERVES 6

14-ounce can tomatoes
1 garlic clove
3 scallions

few drops hot-pepper sauce
salt and freshly ground black pepper

Place all the ingredients in a food processor or blender and pulse for a few seconds until smooth. Season to taste, then pour into an air-tight container and refrigerate for up to 5 days until required.

BARBECUE SALSA

Serve this tasty sauce as an accompaniment to cooked meats or use as a marinade for spareribs.

MAKES ABOUT 3¾ CUPS

1¼ cups tomato ketchup
1 onion, finely chopped
2 tomatoes, peeled, seeded and finely chopped
2 garlic cloves, finely chopped
½-inch piece gingerroot, finely chopped

⅔ cup freshly squeezed orange juice
2 tbsp vegetable oil
3 tbsp soy sauce
3 tbsp honey
1 tsp mustard

Place all the ingredients in a large saucepan with 2 cups water and bring to a boil. Cover and simmer slowly for 20 minutes, stirring occasionally. Cool, cover, and keep in the refrigerator for up to 2 weeks. This also freezes well.

Texan Green Tomato Salsa

This fairly fiery salsa should be served chilled. Make it milder or hotter by altering the amounts and type of chili you use.

SERVES 8

4 green chilies, seeded and
    finely chopped
4 green tomatoes, roughly
    chopped
2 onions, roughly chopped

2 garlic cloves, finely chopped
1 tbsp chopped fresh oregano,
    or ½ tbsp dried
salt and freshly ground black
    pepper

❶ Place the chilies, tomatoes, onions, garlic, and about 1¼ cups water in a saucepan and bring to a boil. Cover and simmer for 30 minutes, stirring occasionally, until thick and pulpy.
❷ Strain the mixture through a fine nonmetallic strainer, then stir in the garlic, oregano, and salt and pepper to taste. Cover and chill up to 5 days until required.

WATERMELON SALSA

Bring out the flavor of plain
broiled or roasted seafood, such as lobster or scallops,
with this salsa.

SERVES 6

1 small cucumber
1¼ cups diced watermelon flesh
1 small red onion, thinly sliced
1 tbsp chopped fresh mint
1 tbsp snipped fresh chives
*1 small red chili, seeded and
  finely chopped*

*1 small garlic clove, finely
  chopped*
freshly squeezed juice of 1 lime
*salt and freshly ground black
  pepper*

❶ Slice the cucumber in half lengthwise, then slice each half to make semicircles. Place them in a bowl with the watermelon, red onion, mint, chives, chili, garlic, and lime juice.

❷ Season to taste and serve immediately, or cover and chill for up to one day.

BARBECUED SALSA *WITH* HERBED

OIL DRESSING

This makes a delicious outdoor meal served with baked
potatoes and a spoonful of sour cream.

SERVES 6

4 corn cobs
8 tomatoes, quartered
2 red onions, quartered

HERBED OIL DRESSING

4 tbsp olive oil
2 tbsp balsamic vinegar
*2 tbsp chopped fresh tarragon
  seasoning*

❶ Begin by making the herbed oil–stir together the oil, vinegar, herbs, salt and pepper.

❷ Brush the corn cobs with the dressing and place on the barbecue for 20 to 30 minutes. Remove the kernels.

❸ Thread the tomatoes and onions onto skewers and brush with the oil. Barbecue for 15 to 20 minutes until tender.

❹ Transfer the kernels, onions, and tomatoes to a large bowl. Pour over the remaining dressing.

Watermelon Salsa

CRANBERRY KETCHUP

This sweet-and-sour ketchup makes a tasty accompaniment to fried chicken.

MAKES ABOUT 3¾ CUPS

2 pounds fresh cranberries
2½ cups golden raisins
2 cups red-wine vinegar
2 to 2¼ cups soft brown sugar

2 tsp ground allspice
1 tsp salt
1 tsp ground cinnamon

❶ Place all the ingredients in a large saucepan and bring to a boil, stirring until the sugar dissolves. Cover and simmer for 1 hour, stirring occasionally.
❷ Strain the mixture through a fine nonmetallic strainer, then pour immediately into hot, sterilized bottles. Seal (page 10) and store until required.

PESTO SALSA

Using the same basic ingredients as the Italian pasta sauce of the same name, this Californian salsa is best served with fish or poultry. Use to fill the cavities of 4 small fish or make deep incisions in 4 chicken breasts and spread the salsa thickly on top before barbecuing or broiling.

SERVES 4

4 tbsp pine nuts
2 large garlic cloves, finely chopped
1 small red chili, seeded and finely chopped
2 handfuls fresh basil, finely chopped

2 tbsp freshly grated Parmesan or Pecorino cheese
4 tbsp extra-virgin olive oil
freshly squeezed juice and grated peel of 1 lemon
salt and freshly ground black pepper

❶ Place the pine nuts in a nonstick skillet and dry-fry for 3 to 5 minutes until golden. Use a heavy knife to chop them finely.

❷ Place the nuts in a bowl with the garlic, chili, basil, cheese, olive oil, and lemon juice and peel and season well with salt and plenty of black pepper. Use immediately, or cover and chill for up to 2 hours.

INDEX

ACKNOWLEDGEMENTS

Key: (a) above   (b) below

David Grant/Ace 7, John Lambie/Ace 9, Michael Freeman 10, Mauritius/Ace 11, Heinz USA 12 (a), Robert Opie 12 (b), David Kerwin/Ace 14, Pictor 16, Ben Simmons/Ace 17, Pictor 19, Paul Craven/Ace 22, Michael Freeman 23, Mark Stevenson/Ace 38, Billie Love Historical Collection 39, Pictor 54, Kevin Phillips/Ace 55, Norman Browne/Ace 66, Michael Freeman 67, Pictor 80, 81, 96, 97 & 112, Pli/Ace 113.
All other photographs are the copyright of Quarto Publishing plc.
Quarto would also like to thank Elizabeth David Cookshop, The Piazza, Covent Garden, London WC2E 8RA for supplying equipment for photography.